Some of My Personal WinSights into God

REFLECTIONS ON THE GOODNESS OF GOD

MALCOLM BLOWES

ISBN 979-8-89428-787-4 (paperback)
ISBN 979-8-89428-788-1 (digital)

Christian Faith Publishing
832 Park Avenue
Meadville, PA 16335
www.christianfaithpublishing.com

Printed in the United States of America

To Jesus Christ, my Savior

CONTENTS

ACKNOWLEDGMENTS

With enormous thanks to my loving, remarkably patient wife, Phyllis.

Also, thanks to pastors Rueben and Hazel Frankland for revealing to me the Word of Life teaching.

A big thanks as well to Ruby Kehayias for editing my atrocious grammar.

INTRODUCTION

So why did I choose the subject and title of this book I have authored as *Some of My Personal Winsights into God: Reflections on the Goodness of God?*

Well, it was written primarily to record a list of just a few of the true testimonies that I have experienced in my long walk with God as a born-again Christian.

My hope is that many readers will find, through these pages, lasting peace, joy, factual revelation, and the truth about our Creator God within their own lives as they read each chapter. By looking deeper into these testimonies, we can learn how we can also get to grips with faith and learn from them.

One popular songwriter proclaimed, "Christianity will go. It will vanish and shrink. I do not know what will go first, rock 'n' roll or Christianity." He claimed his band at that time was more popular than Jesus Christ. He went on to further say, "Jesus was all right, but his disciples were thick and ordinary. It is them twisting it that ruins it for me."

I'm sad to report that the particular famous spokesperson is deceased, but Jesus is still alive, saving souls, and Christianity is still growing in great strides, stronger and stronger, throughout many parts of the world.

I thank the Lord Jesus Christ that I had an encounter with full-time missionaries Eddie and the late Annette Martens when they were on their way to Tunisia. It was through them that the enlightenment of the good news (the gospel) convinced me that I needed to be born again and that my old, messed-up, debauched life could be washed away by the precious blood of Jesus Christ.

They went on to enlighten me that it had nothing to do with my past, present, or future and even however good or bad I had been. They assured me that I couldn't have done anything bad enough to keep me out of heaven or good enough to get me into heaven. It was all because of not what I did, but what God did.

I knew deep down I had been rebellious, although at the time, I only thought I was just doing what everyone else of my generation seemed to be going along with. They explained that it was not about anything I had thought, said, or done, but about what Jesus had done for me by taking my place on the cross. It was the first time I had ever heard such a thing, although, by then, I was in my midthirties.

I suddenly realized that it was my thoughts, words, and actions that had chained me into a pattern, and I was in a prison of my own making. It was only after giving my heart to Jesus by speaking a prayer and repenting that I became free of my womanizing and cussing of God's name. I was set free from nicotine and alcohol addictions and a crazy, uncontrolled temper, to name but a few. I learned for the first time that God is a good God, not what traditional religion had taught me!

> Or do you despise the riches of His goodness, forbearance, and longsuffering, not knowing that the goodness of God leads you to repentance? (Romans 2:4)

What a mess I left behind! Don't get me wrong; I still haven't arrived yet. I've still got some way to go in my relationship with God, but I've left the dock and I've set my sails to be on my way and press toward the goal for the prize, praise God!

I received God's Holy Spirit to live inside at that time, and just a few months later, I discovered and received a second experience when the wind of the Holy Spirit came, not in me, but on me, which gave me new power to shake off my current generation's philosophical confessions.

I now saw that so many things I had believed and accepted were all just a great big fat lie. That my bad thoughts, words, and actions were actually there to trap me into a life of fear, depression, physical sickness, poverty, lack, debt, dissatisfaction, and eventual complete unfulfillment that led to death.

After seeing a remarkable change in me, my wife Phyllis became a Christian six months later. God then was able to restore our marriage and its lost trust and started to teach me how to be a better husband and father. I really cannot visualize where I would be today, thirty-nine years later, if I had not accepted Jesus as my Savior. I'm sure I would be divorced, in some prison, or maybe dead.

> O my people, listen to my instructions. Open your ears to what I am saying, for I will speak to you in a parable. I will teach you hidden lessons from our past, stories [songs] we have heard and known, stories [songs] our ancestors handed down to us. (Psalm 88:1–3 NLT, my emphasis added).

Just a brief added note before you start to read: please be assured that although some of these testimonies carry a seemingly incredible forceful message and may even seem far-fetched, all the accounts listed in this book were experienced personally either by myself, my family, or my friends, and I affirm that they are the absolute, amazing truth to the goodness of a supernatural Creator, Father God!

CHAPTER 1

God Is in the Specifics!

Let us start off this book with an encouraging word from Jesus in the scriptures: "Therefore, do not worry, saying, 'What shall we eat?' or 'What shall we drink?' or 'What shall we wear?' For after all these things the Gentiles look for. For your heavenly Father knows that you need all these things. But look for first the kingdom of God and His righteousness, and all these things shall be added to you" (Matthew 6:32).

First, let us notice from the preceding verse that our worrying over a particularly disturbing situation, however big or small, never helps the situation but actually makes circumstances worse. It is because as we speak out our bad thoughts, they will often turn into our actions of fear through lack of understanding of the power in our words when spoken.

This above Bible verse really is a reminder that we can often get distracted, even by the little *things*, and speak negative, and creative words over ourselves and others. There's an old saying by the novelist Gustave Flaubert that "the devil is in the details," but that is often not the actual truth. The reality is that God is much more often in the specific details in our lives.

One time when we were living in the Republic of Slovakia as missionaries, my wife Phyllis and our daughter Holly had to make a quick bus ride visit back to England. While she was there, she needed to get to a certain location. So she contacted one of our close

Christian friends and asked if they could oblige and give her and our daughter a lift in their car.

They responded positively, but when John Turner, the husband, came to pick them up from other friends where they were staying, he seemed rather agitated and not at all his usual cheerful self. Phyllis was concerned that she was the cause of his upset because she had asked him to be her chauffeur for the evening as she was without transport.

When she asked him what was troubling him, he then went on to tell her why he was so upset! He was a little embarrassed because, as he related his story, he felt it sounded almost trivial, but it had, in fact, been a huge personal disappointment for him earlier that very day.

He had earlier seen an expensive used camera in a store window that he had wanted for some years and had asked the storekeeper to hold it for him until he was paid at the end of the week. The proprietor had agreed to do so, but disappointingly, when John returned to the store to redeem it earlier that day, the store owner hadn't kept his promise—the camera had been sold to someone else.

He had prayed and really believed he was going to have that camera and said he felt like God himself, rather than the shop owner, had let him down and he was having real difficulty getting over it. My wife reached into her bag, pulled out a camera that her brother-in-law had just given her the day before, and said to our friend, "I don't know anything about cameras, but I was given this yesterday and was told that it was a somewhat expensive one. You are more than welcome to have it."

He had a look of amazement on his face as he declared that it was the exact same make and model of camera that he had been after. Tears filled his eyes when he realized that God hadn't let him down at all and in fact had had a better plan! This camera was without cost—yes, free, gratis. It was a joy for Phyllis to be in the right place at the right time and to be part of God's plan in someone else's life.

So we must be careful not to allow the little or even bigger things that seem to go amiss to rob us of our joy and victory. When I feel worried and anxious about a certain situation that I'm having to deal with, I read and meditate on the following scriptures and others like them. Not just once, but many times over until they become a part of me, because "faith comes by hearing, and hearing by the word of God" (Romans 10:17).

Notice, it says by hearing and the need to hear over and over again, not just by having heard it once. God is in the details and has all the answers for our problems and wants to give us a way of escape. Start to speak your faith into that situation, and "you shall have what you say" (Mark 11:23).

We need to start calling "those things which do not exist as though they did" (Romans 4:17), confessing that "My God shall supply all your need according to His riches in glory by Christ Jesus" (Philippians 4:19), declaring with King David, "The Lord is my shepherd; I shall not want" (Psalm 23:1) and proclaiming that I am going to "let patience have its perfect work, that you may be perfect and complete, lacking nothing" (James 1:4).

> For I know the thoughts that I think toward you, says the Lord, thoughts of peace and not evil, to give you a future and a hope. Then you will call upon Me and go and pray to Me, and I will listen to you. And you will seek Me and find Me when you search for Me with all your heart. (Jeremiah 29:11–13)

> Be anxious for nothing, but in everything by prayer and supplication, with thanksgiving, let your requests be made known to God. (Philippians 4:6)

> Cast your burden on the Lord, and He shall sustain you; He shall never allow the righteous to be moved. (Psalm 55:22)

> Fear not, for I am with you; be not dismayed, for I am your God. I will strengthen you. Yes, I will help you. I will uphold you with My righteous right hand. (Isaiah 41:10)

It's a medically proven fact that stress, worry, fear, and anxiety can have major negative consequences on our physical and mental health and arrest our natural immune system, which protects us from sicknesses, diseases, infirmities, viruses, and infections. It may even shorten our lifespan. Allowing severe, continuous stress will take a physical toll and can damage your body in many ways, affecting everything from your heart to your immune system and your necessary sleep.

Jesus tells us that it is ineffective to worry about what we eat and drink, what we wear, or even about tomorrow, for worry has never changed any situation. "For you cannot make a single hair white or black" (Matthew 5:36).

Worry, fear, and anxiety are the enemies of our souls. What does the Bible say about that enemy, the thief Satan? He comes to us to kill, steal, and destroy (John 10:10a).

Our victory over life's problems is to put our hope and trust in God. He will never leave us or forsake us. Let us set the Lord always before us because he is at our right hand, and we shall not be moved. Therefore, our hearts are glad, our glory rejoices, and our flesh also shall rest in hope (Psalm 16:8–9).

Thank God that we don't have to be moved. The Lord is our strength and source. No matter what comes our way, he is with us. He is our shield and our strong tower. "The name of the Lord is a strong tower: the righteous run to it and are safe" (Proverbs 18:10).

The Lord is the anchor of our souls. When the winds of adversity blow, if we are rooted in Jesus Christ, we can stand. He will not suffer our foot to be moved. He will teach us how to stand strong and make wise choices. The Lord helps us walk in the truth of His Word and get beyond our feelings. He supplies open doors for us and shows us how to take advantage of them. Even when hindrances arise, He shows us how to turn them around and make them into opportunities.

Even when we feel all kinds of adversity against us, we should not be moved. Our outcome in Christ is always victory. Don't be moved from your position of faith. Know that the promises of God are sure. He will not fail us.

In any situation, an effective fervent prayer would be like this:

> Father, thank You for positioning me for victory. Help me to stand firm on Your truth and in Your ways no matter what I face in life. "For whatsoever is born of God overcomes the world: and this is the victory that overcomes the world, even our faith" (1 John 5:4 KJV).

When we put our trust and confidence in God, he always causes us to come into victory. "Now thanks be to God who always leads us in triumph in Christ, and through us diffuses the fragrance of His knowledge in every place" (2 Corinthians 2:14).

A famous musician composed a song, "Blow Away." The song is by the late ex-Beatle lead guitarist George Harrison. It's one of the most admired soundtracks from his solo career. Harrison says that the song arose from his emotional state of disappointment and shortcoming resulting from a leaking roof at his Friar Park mansion in the English county of Oxfordshire and from pondering a rainstorm from an outbuilding on his vast property.

Even as a nonbelieving Bible Christian, he came to realize that, in yielding to the predicament, he was merely worsening it. This state of affairs Jesus deliberates and confirms in the Gospels: "This evil nation is like a man had by a demon. For if the demon leaves, it goes into the deserts for a while, seeking rest but finding none. Then it says, 'I will return to the man I came from.' So, it returns and finds the man's heart clean but empty! Then the demon finds seven other spirits more evil than itself, and all enter the man and live in him. And so, he is worse off than before" (Matthew 12:43–45 TLB).

With this realization, this incident served as a reminder to George Harrison that he, in fact, needed to "*love everybody*" regardless of who they are and should look to be more optimistic. Additionally, he notes that while he initially felt self-conscious about the song, thinking it "so obvious," the track grew on him when he recorded it. Unwittingly, he never knew that God's purposes are greater than our problems.

We could certainly ask ourselves, why would multimillionaire George Harrison feel so concerned and irritated about a leaky roof at just one of his luxury homes? Friar Park is a 120-room Victorian neo-Gothic mansion, with grounds covering about sixty-two acres.

How did George allow himself through disillusionment to write down the words "Day turned black, sky ripped apart, rained for a year till it dampened my heart"? His heart was heavy even though his amassed fortune could have not only fixed his roof but also built him an even bigger mansion without making even a small dent in his vast fortune, and he would not have had to even lift a finger to touch a single bag of cement, a brick, or a tile himself!

American Baptist pastor, evangelist, and author Rick Warren writes that "God is most glorified in us when we are most satisfied in Him. What does that mean for us? That human life is a messy business—a hodgepodge of everything from minor inconveniences to death itself. God is bigger than every single one of those things."

Have you, or have I, ever had feelings of frustration and inadequacy? Have you or I easily let surmountable problems, little difficulties, and the minor cares of this world become an obstruction to our walk of faith with Jesus? Have you or I ever grumbled, murmured, and complained to ourselves at the slow line at the grocery store? Or have we judged the perceived inefficiency of a bank teller serving us? Of course, we all have. It seems so difficult sometimes in not allowing our flesh nature to override our born-again spirit and allow our soul to lose its kindness.

We are commanded as God's children not to take on worry, anxiety, and concerns for our life's problems. Instead, we must "be content with who you are, and don't put on airs. God's strong hand is on you; he'll promote you at the right time. Live carefree before God; he is most careful with you" (1 Peter 5:7 MSG).

We are instructed by God's Word not to be overcome by the problems of credit debts and the lack of finances because they will overwhelm us even when they are really only minor. When we start to recognize to give all we have to God that we may receive all that he has. And what a measure he has to give us! "For every beast of the forest is Mine, and the cattle on a thousand hills. I know all the birds of the mountains, and the wild beasts of the field are Mine" (Psalm 50:10–11).

> The God who holds your breath in His
> hand and owns all your ways. (Daniel 5:23b)

We need, as implied by the deceased Mr. Harrison's song lyrics, to find deliverance, be happy, feel that warmth inside, and let the cares of this world go by. The answer that he discovered is the identical revelation for us all, which is to simply *love*. Which is one of Jesus's names.

Christian charity has to succeed in first loving our merciful heavenly Father and also our neighbors as ourselves. Love will turn all our situations, whether great or minuscule (and us not misguidedly turning to yang from yin). Love will fill our spirit, soul, and body from darkness to light. The difficult situations may not have immediately changed, but our attitude has! "There is no fear in love; but perfect love casts out fear because fear involves torment. But he who fears has not been made perfect in love" (1 John 4:18).

The Platters released a hit song, "Only You," on May 20, 1954, and ex-Beatles drummer Ringo Starr covered this song for his album "Goodnight Vienna" in 1974, at the suggestion of another ex-Beatle, John Lennon. Only the peace God's presence brings can make this world seem right. Only the Holy Spirit can make the darkness bright. He's the one to fill hearts with love. Only the Lord Jesus Christ can make this change in us. For it's true, as the song says, he is our destiny. Only Jesus!

Singer Stevie Wonder wrote and recorded a song titled "Don't You Worry 'bout a Thing." Likewise, God is saying to us, his children, "*Don't you worry about anything,*" because He will be standing on our side when we need to come to him with our problems. Like what's said in Stevie's lyrics, some of us just don't know how to overcome even the smallest of setbacks. We are always reaching out in vain, merely worrying about things that really do not matter and not having much substance.

I am also reminded of another time that God was in the specifics for our immediate needs. Our daughter Holly and our son-in-law Jake have lived full-time in Cameroon, Africa, for over twenty years with their four children, where they have established an orphanage for children in desperate situations and abandoned orphans, and a part-time Bible college under Win Our Nations' banner. They have also started Children's Club. To help fund these ministries, they opened a butcher's shop one time for expatriates, and at various times, car washes, a chicken farm, and a rabbit farm.

Every four years, the family returns to the USA for a six-month furlough, where they travel from coast to coast visiting regular supporters and raising new sponsors by speaking at churches. Each time before they return, they ask us to look out for a large recreational vehicle for them to get ready for when they arrive. With such a vehicle, they save on having to use hotels and restaurants on their cross-country travels. One of the first times was in 2012 when they had a budget maximum of just $7,000. The time for their return was running out, and we were getting a little desperate.

One particular day, we saw a large older Ford Coachman for sale with a price tag of $10,000. It was in a Presbyterian church parking lot with a telephone number attached. We contacted the owners, a pleasant older couple who were church members there. They invited us to their home to check their RV out.

We found it had very low mileage, had been mechanically well maintained, and the interior was still in good condition, with new tires all around. We recognized that this vehicle would meet the needs of the ministry perfectly. The man invited me and my wife to take it out for a test drive. We hadn't gone just a few blocks when the engine started sputtering and missing. I returned it back, telling the owner that there was something wrong with the motor. He became quite hot and bothered, stating there was absolutely nothing wrong with the vehicle. He asked if I knew how to drive. I calmly assured him I had been driving for forty-five years and I also knew how to drive a recreational vehicle.

We returned home disappointed and almost immediately received a telephone call from the RV owner. He wanted to apologize and said that I was correct, it had not been running well and that he had discovered that it was just a blocked fuel filter which he had now replaced. He said it was now working fine and requested us to please come back again.

We returned and felt the need to confess to them that before we take it out again for a test drive, my wife and I want to be completely honest and straightforward with them. We are not trying to scam you, lie to you, or negotiate a different price, but we only had a maximum limit of $7,000 for a vehicle, and if we purchased their RV, we would have to owe them the rest over a time. We said, "So maybe it is not going to work for us and really not worth us taking it out again for a test drive." Yes, we did know the scripture that clearly states, "Owe no one anything except to love one another, for he who loves another has fulfilled the law" (Romans 13:8).

We then had the opportunity to explain in more detail about our overseas ministry and also what the vehicle we were seeking was to be used for. They said, "Take it out again anyway." This gave us hope that maybe they might be willing to come down some on the price. This time the vehicle functioned perfectly, and we returned it back satisfied with it and hoped we could in some way obtain this vehicle. Then we got to discussing the price. They said that while we were out test driving, they had prayed and together discussed it and had decided to *give us the vehicle*! They had just paid $1,000 for the new tires to help sell the vehicle, and if we could just possibly pay for those, which of course we were very pleased to do.

Can you imagine how often this kind of action would happen outside of the kingdom of God and his people! "Every good gift and every perfect gift is from above, and comes down from the Father of lights, with whom there is no variation or shadow of turning" (James 1:17).

Wow, what an incredible God we serve. Our kids and four grandkids put thousands of trouble-free miles on that RV over six months. By having to pay only a fraction for it, they saved their money for gas and groceries. God is so good. Win Our Nations ministry in turn sold the RV after they returned to Cameroon for much-welcomed and needed funds.

> For who has despised the day of small
> things? For these seven rejoice to see the plumb
> line in the hand of Zerubbabel. They are the eyes
> of the Lord, which scan to and fro throughout
> the whole earth. (Zechariah 4:10)

Just before he ascended into heaven, Jesus gave us a math problem that centered on increase. In a comparison, he talked about multiplying new believers. He didn't take on the problem himself. Astonishingly, he left the job up to a group of humans. He left it up to you and me. He said to his disciples, "Go into all the world and preach the gospel to every creature" (Mark 15:16).

To help complete this task, we need to be able to see the people in our lives that need the help of Jesus Christ's presence in their own lives. We need to see who we can share our faith with not only by our words, but by our actions. But that is not always an easy thing for us to do. In order for us to see the needs of these people, we may need to look at their lives through a different lens, through a different perspective. We need to put on polarized glasses.

Differentiated sunglasses are amazing. When you are out on a lake or walking in the woods, these glasses help you to see with more clarity and sharpness. They allow you to be able to see things around you that you could not have seen without them.

Let's look at those suffering, sick, broke, and lost as God sees them. His love for all is unconditional. Don't be moved by any circumstances, however big or small. It is God who is in the details, not the devil. Just believe that and receive it!

The same thing needs to be always happening in our lives. But to gain that new perspective, we need to ask God to give us the spiritual vision of polarized glass. We must ask God to give us extreme insight to be able to see those around us who need Christ in their lives.

Today ask God to give you extreme "winsight." Just say to Him, "God, show me someone in my life that I need to invite to church or share you with." God wants you to be his witness. Look for the people in your life that need him, and then be a witness to what God has done in your life. Help finish God's equation of multiplying new believers.

CHAPTER 2

Getting Back to Basics!

For it pleased the Father that in Him all the fullness should dwell
and by Him to reconcile all things to Himself, by Him, whether
things on earth or things in heaven, having made peace through
the blood of His cross. And you, who once were alienated and
enemies in your mind by wicked works, yet now He has reconciled

—Colossians 1:19–21

Have you ever found yourself being so busy that you haven't gotten time for God? Even for full-time ministers of the gospel,
this is always a great danger for us all. We allow ourselves to get so
wrapped up in business, ministry, finances, just living life, etc.

When we get away from the basic Christian facts of *who* we are
called to have a close relationship with, *where* God has lifted us from,
what He has saved us from, *why* we are where we are today, and *how*
it was accomplished for us at the cross of Calvary, then we start to
suffer defeat in our once-close fellowship with God.

At one time in our lives, my wife Phyllis and I were at a point in
our walk with Jesus when the Christian ministry we were serving had
started to become a real burden to both of us. Extremely long hours
of work with little financial support or little encouragement from our
fellow ministry staff were taking their toll on us.

It was our first time in ministry in the USA, and we felt like a couple of ducks out of water just getting off the banana boat. It was a tough time, to say the least. We were in a spiritual slump and had so little time and energy to do anything about it. We thanked God for our church, which was a huge blessing, and could hardly wait for Sundays to come around and enjoy the freedom of worshiping the Lord in the beauty of holiness. It was our lifeline! Maybe worshiping Jesus is where we ought to be all of the time, at least once a day.

Both of us were assigned to different departments, and as I was working nights in the print shop, working twelve-hour shifts, we had become like passing ships in the night. As I left for work, she was returning from work, swapping out a warm bed from the other. It doesn't take a rocket scientist to figure out that this is not a healthy routine for any marriage! So often in the past, we had romanticized that it would be like heaven on earth working and serving God in full-time ministry, living by faith, trusting God alone! Sadly, that can often be far from reality, what with having to reach deadlines, constant financial pressure, dealing with the carnal actions of colleagues, and generally not showing each other the love God intended us to show.

One Saturday night, while lying in bed, we were not able to sleep. We were talking in the early hours of the morning with the moon as bright as day streaming into the window of the ministry's broken-down old trailer we called home. I mentioned that it would be so nice to go for a walk on the beach in the moonlight and pray.

Phyllis replied, "Well, why not? Let's do it then!"

We headed for the beach, which is about a twenty-minute drive away. When we got there, we found out that there was nowhere to park as there were restrictions after midnight. We kept driving around for quite a while until I finally found somewhere to park. As we walked over the boardwalk and onto the beach, the moon was so bright that we could see everything like daylight. Right there, as we walked toward the area of beach where we had decided to park, someone had earlier in the day drawn an enormous cross in the sand. When we saw it, both our hearts just melted, and we cried in each other's arms.

The Lord had supernaturally directed us to this particular spot out of all the miles and miles of beaches to just say to us, "This is what it is all about—the cross of Calvary, the divine exchange." It was a holy moment, a reminder that Jesus must be our focus, and a notice to get back on track, to live a life of worship to him, to dwell and thrive in his kingdom, and to bring glory to his name.

Whoever drew that gigantic cross that day was, maybe unknowingly, inspired by the Holy Spirit to do it. They may never know this side of heaven how it affected our lives at exactly the right time. It was just like God himself put his loving arms around us and said, "There, there, it's going to be okay," and of course, it was. We successfully completed our three-year commitment with that particular ministry and moved on to better things.

If you are experiencing that you are too busy even for God at the moment, then get back to the cross of Jesus Christ today. That is where we first found our salvation, through his spilled blood. That is where we can still find our deliverance from depression, fear, and doubt. It is through Jesus's sacrifice only that we find supernatural healing for our bodies. At the cross, we will find satisfaction, happiness, prosperity, success, and victory over sin and the world.

Join me today by getting back to the basics of our faith. Put your trust back in Jesus. It is him and only him who is our Savior, our Friend, our great High Priest, our Brother, our coming King of kings and Lord of lords, and our only way to God.

The Lord hears the cry of the blameless. "The righteous cry and the Lord hears and delivers them out of all their trouble" (Psalm 34:17).

When Christ comes into our life, all that stuff that had us in bondage has to loose us and let us go. It cannot hold on to us anymore. Now we can reach forward and grab for the new. The old has no power left to hold on to us. No matter what we were into before Christ, once Jesus comes in, those things no longer have any authority over us.

There is a force called righteousness that is now at work in us. That power pulls us and causes us to want to do the right thing. We are now a righteous people, so make that commitment to live a righteous life. What does it mean to be righteous? Righteousness is right and unrighteousness is wrong. "For the righteous Lord loveth righteousness; his countenance doth behold the upright" (Psalm 11:7).

The Lord looks after the righteous. If we want to get over the abundant blessings, let's make up our minds to live right. Blessings will come upon us and overtake us. God will show favor toward us. Make it your purpose to live right. "The Lord redeems the soul of His servants: and none of them that trust in him shall be desolate" (Psalm 34:22). Why not say to yourselves aloud a few times right now, "I am righteousness of God in Christ Jesus."

Some Other Related Verses

For God so loved the world that He gave His only begotten Son, that whoever believes in Him should not perish but have everlasting life. (John 3:16)

Nor is there salvation in any other, for there is no other name under heaven given among men by which we must be saved. (Acts 4:12)

For there is one God and one Mediator between God and man, the Man Christ Jesus. (1 Timothy 2:5)

Cast your burden on the Lord, and He shall sustain you; He shall never allow the righteous to be moved. (Psalm 55:22)

CHAPTER 3

Fishermen Sow for a Catch

Do all things without complaining and disputing, that
you may become blameless and harmless, children of
God without fault in the midst of a crooked and perverse
generation, among whom you shine as lights in the world.

—Philippians 2:14–15

In November 1998, our daughter Holly took Phyllis and me to Orlando International Airport for a flight to Gatwick, London, for the first leg of our mission trip to South Africa. We were flying Virgin Atlantic for the first time, and we were excited as we had heard such good things about that particular airline. We had our own two seventy-pound duffels and a guitar, two stuffed backpacks, plus two seventy-pound ministry duffels. Unfortunately, it turned out to be a most difficult flight to London.

We had had a good Bible study together when we first were seated on the Boeing 747, and we had been studying the above verse: "Do all things without complaining and disputing" (Philippians 2:14).

After a particularly difficult and stressful day at the ministry headquarters, we were convicted by the Word of God, which we had just read, and we decided to confess quietly aloud to God about our inward, although unuttered, complaining and disputing about other persons in the ministry. We decided to repent to God and made a vow to drop our ungodly behavior as Christian witnesses.

As so often happens when we have made a new commitment and promise to God, we were immediately tested to see if it is genuine. It was amazing! The man directly in front of me on the airplane had a broken seat that came back too far. He couldn't keep it in the upright position. The seat of the woman behind us was by the back lavatories and couldn't recline, so she wouldn't allow me to recline mine. I had about eighteen inches between the tops of their seats and had to sit bolt upright the whole journey. When I had my tray table down, it stuck in my stomach. When I politely mentioned this to a flight attendant, she informed us that it was my own fault for not reporting it when we were still on the ground.

We were on the plane over an hour and a half before we were offered a drink, and they only had warm canned drinks. My overhead light didn't work nor was the light to call the attendant, who had a particularly annoying voice and tone. She just agreed with everything people pointed out and said, "Yes, I know, it's terrible isn't it." Connotations of BBC's TV's *Fawlty Towers* came to mind.

There were other trivial things like just my meal being without individual salt and pepper portions, the milk carton being empty when I opened it, and there being no sodas to drink with the meal because we were supposed to drink wine, and we would have to wait until she had served the rest of the plane." My bread roll was dry and rock hard, although Phyllis's was fine. All these things came to appraise our vows to the Lord to the limit. It was two and a half hours before we ate at all, and they didn't clear the trays for at least another hour after we had finished. People were lined up at the toilets as we were landing because they hadn't been able to get out of their seats, because all the meal trays weren't cleared.

Toward the end of the flight, because the lady in front complained so much, the flight attendant voluntarily started to distribute a handful of official complaint forms that she had been asked for by other passengers, which many of them took. We were each offered one as well, which we both refused. Can you believe that within five and a half hours of making our vow to the Lord Jesus never again to complain, grumble, and protest, we were offered a form for us to mark a list of complaints on! Praise God, we never lapsed in all that test, and we laughed and laughed as it all unfolded. Be sure whatever you declare for God, you will be evaluated on.

To continue with the significance of this story, we landed at Gatwick Airport at 9:00 a.m. with very little sleep and caught a bus to Heathrow Airport with all our luggage and arrived around noon. The grass was white with frost when we landed, and we could see our breath when we got outside, and for a Florida-based resident, it was positively enchanting. We had to wait until 9:00 p.m. for our flight to South Africa. So we walked to Terminal 1 and had (real) fish 'n' chips for lunch at Harry Ramsden's. What can I say? They were delicious!

When we took off on our second Virgin flight, it couldn't have been more different compared to the earlier one. It was an Airbus 320, and we got seats by an exit and had all the leg room in the world. The food was delicious, and our flight attendants were so pleasant. When they asked us to share why we were going, they even gave us a bunch of Virgin Atlantic schoolbags for the African kids we would be working with in South Africa. If we keep obeying God's Word, it will all turn out right in the end (confirmation comes by studying the whole Book of Job).

The moral of this true account is that it was interesting to note that, if we were only going as far as London, England, on that first flight and had judged Virgin Atlantic airlines by that primary experience, what a miscarriage of justice that would have been. As our second flight proved why Virgin Atlantic has such a good reputation. So a question we must all ask ourselves as Christians is this: when new Christians meet with others for the first time, are they seeing the worst or the best in the body of Christ through us? If we had not been in transit, but had ended our journey at Gatwick, we might have agreed with the lady in the seat behind, "to never fly with this airline again."

Wouldn't it be too sad for words if others' first impressions toward us might keep them from knowing the real love of Jesus and all that the kingdom of God and eternity have to offer! Our due season is here, so "let us not be weary in well doing; for in due season, we shall reap if we faint not" (Galatians 6:9).

God will deliver us from our weariness when we are losing heart by reminding us that in due season, we shall reap if we faint not. Due season is God's set and appointed time for our lives when we receive His reward. Remember, seedtime and harvest shall never cease. After you have sown, always expect the harvest, whether for good or bad.

Our appointed time is not just a reward to be received when we get to heaven. There are great rewards to be received right here on earth. There are great doors of favor and blessings that God wants to open for us which no man can close. Sing, clap, dance, run, rejoice, and shout today, for our actual appointed time is here.

The fruit from our service, resisting temptations, clean living, prayer, and all of the seed we have sown is ready for harvest, so continue to sow. We will not give up! We will not even think about quitting. Our due season is now. God is faithful, and he will do all that he has promised. Our appointed season has arrived.

The apostle Paul tells us the same thing in his testimony of his meeting with others for the first time: "To the Jews I became as a Jew, that I might win Jews; to those who are under the law, as under the law, that I might win those who are under the law; to those who are without law, as without law (not being without law toward God, but under law toward Christ), that I might win those who are without law; to the weak I became as weak, that I might win the weak. I have become all things to all men, that I might by all means save some. Now this I do for the gospel's sake, that I may be partaker of it with you" (1 Corinthians 9:20–24).

Declare, "Let me receive the fruit of your sowing." And say, "This is my appointed season." God is faithful, and he will do all that he has promised. Our appointed season is here. Let us receive the fruit of our sowing. Let's declare "This is my appointed season." "To everything there is a season, and a time to every purpose under the heaven" (Ecclesiastes 3:1).

God is going to be bringing new folks and opportunities into our lives almost daily. How will they first perceive us? As religious pious hypocrites, as worldly Christians, or as interested, loving, and caring folks?

Repentance is the answer to our prayers for many things. For Jesus said, "Repent, for the kingdom of heaven is at hand." (Matthew 4:17).

CHAPTER 4

Body Impact

And this gospel of the Kingdom will be preached
in the entire world as a witness to all the
nations and then the end will come.

—Matthew 24:14

What an incredible concept it is that the God who created the whole universe has entrusted us (his body) with the task of reaching the world for Jesus. If we are eager to see the Lord's return, we need to take his words seriously enough to participate and be actively involved in making the Gospel relevant to every tribe, tongue, and nation.

I believe that the very heart of God is missions, and that he is calling us, his body, to understand his amazing passion for his creation—for the lost, broken-hearted, and the lonely people of this world. I have been so blessed in my life to have visited many nations of the world and fellowship with believers and know that we are all brothers and sisters of the same family. It is because we have the same Father. We look different, we talk different, our customs and culture are unique to each of us, and maybe even our very lives are very diverse, but we are all one if Jesus Christ is our Lord and Savior.

I remember one time in particular when our family were missionaries in the Republic of Slovakia. Our family, being very traditionally English and out of our element, arranged a gospel outreach in the town square and invited a Christian Hungarian rap group to come and perform and share the good news. We had never put on such a different program or even thought about such a thing before. "Christian *rap*," what is that!

Through that outreach, among the many that responded to our appeal for prayer was one young Slovak man who heard the music, was intrigued, and came to the meeting we held in the town hall that evening. He was actually on his way to a bar with a friend, was unemployed, and had just finished a marijuana joint. He heard the truth of the gospel that night and gave his heart to Jesus and has never been the same since. He got filled with the Holy Spirit, and over thirty years later, he now has a wife (I performed the marriage ceremony) and two children. He can now speak English fluently and has a good occupation in the west of England, where he has moved with his family. They are actively involved in a church there and use their time and finances to spread the gospel around the world.

That same evening, a Roma (Gypsy) youth gave over a revolver gun when we prayed for him. Could we have unknowingly also saved others' physical lives that night? That is the body of Christ in action!

Every one of us has come to the saving knowledge of Jesus Christ because someone else was on a mission to tell the truth of the gospel to us. I thank God that someone told me that I could be saved, to be "born again" and have a brand-new life on this earth, and that I would now spend eternity in heaven with Jesus.

How can anyone be part of this task? This may be a question that you have never asked yourself or even considered, but hopefully you will now. There are three ways we can all get involved in missions.

One way: *pray*. There are many resources that will help you to pray for the nations, such as *Operation World: When We Pray God Works* by Patrick Johnson and Jason Mandryk. Visit their website and learn much more. Adopt a particular country or a people group. God had put on our family's hearts to pray daily for Czechoslovakia as the communist regimes were falling apart and the Russian soldiers were leaving. This was long before we believed that we would ever go there in person.

Second way: *give.* There are many ways to give. We can contribute financially to help support an overseas missionary family or an individual missionary on a regular basis. We can provide for someone going on a short mission trip. We can give of our time to write a card or email to encourage them. Collect clothes (not your old castoffs; give like King David, who gave his best). Another way is to give gifts and candy for the kids for a team to take with them. I have found that children all over the world love candy. You could support an overseas orphan monthly. For example, visit the author's website at winournations.com or another similar mission groups online for more information about this.

A third way: *go.* If you are physically able to go, then go; this is the best way. No photographs or videos can accurately convey what a country is truly like. We need to smell the smells and hear the noises for ourselves. Experience how the majority of the world struggle in such dire poverty and hardship and let your heart be touched. Thirty percent of the world's population doesn't have access to clean drinking water. That may not seem too high, but it represents nearly four billion people. They need help. Overseas missions can greatly assist them. We have dug wells and built WC outhouse latrines in India.

In this generation, we have at our fingertips more ways than ever to complete the task, such as the Internet, satellite television, movies, multimedia, radio, books, and even the feared AI. We can even travel by plane mostly anywhere in the world within twenty-four hours! It's amazing to me to be in India watching the God Channel and seeing the clear gospel being presented without restriction.

As believers, we need to be actively involved in bringing about the Lord's return and have a global view for the lost.

> Because lawlessness will abound, the love of many will grow cold. But he who endures to the end shall be saved. And this gospel of the kingdom will be preached in all the world as a witness to all the nations, and then the end will come. (Matthew 24:13–14)

If we understand these verses correctly, we can see that getting the job done will not be without its many problems. But nothing should distract us from the great commission that the Lord has given to us. Missions are all about reaching the lost for Jesus Christ and the kingdom of God. We can expand it one soul at a time.

Even when we take communion as the body of Christ, we are told to remember him until he returns. I have had the great opportunity to be involved in taking communion with the body in many different nations and this verse always comes to mind:

> For as often as you eat this bread and drink
> this cup, you proclaim the Lord's death till He
> comes. (1 Corinthians 11:26)

CHAPTER 5

Cultural Impact

> To the weak I became as weak,
> that I might win the weak. I have become all things
> to all men that I might by all means save some.
>
> —1 Corinthians 9:22

It is no great revelation to anyone who has been around for a while that, just like me, they can observe that our world and mostly all that is in it have changed dramatically in the last fifty years.

If our great-grandparents could return to earth today and witness our great strides and discoveries in air, land, sea, and space travel, what would they think? In medical and scientific fields—what with all the DNA and technological advancements—they would probably think they were looking at an alien planet out in space. Even in the last ten years, there have been enormous changes in such areas as communications and knowledge and in so many other areas of life.

Take a look at today's youth culture as just one example. If we are to make an impact on our world for Jesus, we must be prepared to change our thinking and methods of how we present the good news (gospel) of Jesus Christ.

The apostle Paul states in this same above chapter that although he is free, he makes himself a servant to all that he might win the more. He says that "to the Jews, he became a Jew as under the law, that he might win those under the law. To those without the law as though without law [though he was still under the law of Christ] that he might win them" (1 Corinthians 9:20). He goes on to say that he does all this for the gospel's sake.

As the timeworn hymn by Arabella Katherine Hankey states, telling the old, old story of the saving gospel of Jesus Christ, the message of his death and his love never changes. But how we go about sharing it must change toward the cultural group we wish to share it with.

Here is just one small personal example. The first time our family went to live full-time on the mission field in Eastern Europe, we looked around to lease a big house and a western vehicle. The same as we had been used to in the west. The problem was that we had been called to work among the very poor, downtrodden, and despised Roma (Gypsy) community. We quickly realized that if we were to reach them, then we needed to rent a tiny apartment of the type which they all lived in and drive a Škoda or Lada car, which they had, and not wear too expensive Western clothes.

This was the only way we were going to identify in any way with them. We also saw we needed to learn and understand their language and be part of their isolated community, which we did with a reasonable measure of success. In fact, much more than did the resident Christian community living in their country that wouldn't adapt at all for them.

The old British nineteenth-century missionary ways of ministering and getting the natives into western clothes and speaking English and living according to their culture probably wasn't always very successful then either.

By the same requirement, if I wished to reach big businessmen in New York, then I would need to wear an expensive Armani suit, Gucci shoes, rent an expensive apartment, and drive a Lexus, Audi, or Jaguar car for them to identify with me for what I wanted to communicate to them.

We cannot be too far above and also too far below or too modern or moreover too old-fashioned from those we are called to witness to and live among and are desiring to reach for Jesus.

Sometimes the only thing holding us back from fulfilling God's destiny for our lives is our own resistance to change. The apostle

Peter states in his second letter, "Grow in the grace and knowledge of our Lord and Savior Jesus Christ" (2 Peter 3:18).

When a young couple is first married, it is a time when they are free to do almost anything together that they please. But when the babies start to come along, then life changes dramatically for them. They can't just go and do whatever they want anymore. Their beautiful tidy home becomes a mess. There appears vomit down their clothes, and smelly diapers always seem to need changing, and noisy sleepless nights appear. They must start to think about investing in someone other than just themselves.

For us on a personal level as Christians, it is all about change. I know for me, and I think for most men and women, the natural attitude is that we do not like or embrace change. We like the way things are and how they have always been. In our fellowships, many of the congregation still like the old hymns better than the newer songs.

We resist when it is time for the fellowship to move to bigger premises because "I grew up in that lovely old building my grandpa helped to build."

Church growth will always bring in the unlovely spiritual babies that are noisy and may even be smelly and will disrupt our comfortable way of life, just like babies do in a family. It will always stretch us to make a change. That's how God works in our lives as we submit to change, line upon line, precept upon precept, glory unto glory.

I am reminded of some years back when my wife and I were booked to go to a three-day ministers' conference in Fort Worth, Texas. I reserved the hotel and hired a car online and then looked for airplane tickets. The problem was I couldn't find seats together on that particular airline's flight. So I telephoned the company and was politely told that they could do nothing to help me right then but to ask at the departures ticketing desk, and they would assist me there.

When we arrived, I was told "Sorry, I can't do anything here. You will have to ask at the gate They will help you there."

At the gate, I explained that I was right at the back of the airplane and my wife was right at the front. We were a whole plane length away from each other, and I asked to be seated together. The lady at the gate desk told me, "Sorry, but we have a full plane," and she could not or would not help me at all. She advised, "Maybe someone will be willing to switch with you on the aircraft."

I began to feel that old, unredeemed, dead man which was once alive in me start to try and rise up again. It told me that I had paid just as much as everyone else for this flight, maybe even more. I had booked my tickets long ago, probably before most of the other passengers had even purchased theirs.

This dead man inside me tried to rise up and said to me, "Complain, make a fuss. It's the squeaky wheel that gets the oil. She will then have to move someone else!"

Praise God that the Spirit of the Lord in the redeemed me suddenly took over, spoke to me, and got my attention, reminding me that, "if My people who are called by My name will humble themselves…" (2 Chronicles 7:14). And then another scripture reminded me that, "God resists the proud, but gives grace to the humble" (James 4:6). I then recognized that I still needed to change in some areas of my life! So we both entered the plane together and accepted our far-off economy seats.

As I made my way to the very back of the aircraft, right by the bulkhead and the last row of three seats, I saw they were occupied in the window and center seats by two middle-aged African American ladies. The lonely aisle seat was still empty and waiting for me.

Soon after takeoff, the lady next to me got out a book and started to read. I deciphered its title out of the corner of my eye, and it was a book by Pastor Bill Winston from Chicago. I asked her, "Excuse me, but are you by any chance both together and Christians?"

By her reply, I could tell she was from the Caribbean Islands. "Yes," she replied, "I am a pastor of a small church in Brooklyn, New York, and this is my fellow traveler and one of our church elders."

We talked for some time, and then I asked, "You both wouldn't by any chance be going to attend the ministers' conference?"

They replied that they were. I asked which hotel they had booked. It was at Fossil Creek, northwest of Fort Worth, and was in the same area as our own hotel. I asked how they were getting there, as it is over thirty miles from the airport, to which she replied, "The Lord knows these things."

I immediately replied, "Yes, he does."

I could see the Holy Spirit all over this. I told them that after we land they should go retrieve their luggage and wait outside arrivals. We would pick them up. "We'll ride the shuttle together to get to our hired car and then give you a ride to your hotel." The ladies looked at each other with a knowing smile.

On the way to the hotel, I asked them how they were getting to the ministers' conference each day, as it was sixteen miles from their hotel. She replied again, "The Lord knows these things." Again, I replied that we would pick them both up at 8:00 a.m. outside their hotel and give them a ride to the conference and bring them back each day. They started to just rejoice in the car.

These two dear sisters had by faith booked flights and a hotel and left the rest of the details to God. What a witness for us, stepping out in belief like that. God had arranged the whole thing, and only my arrogance could have delayed it. To have cultural impact, we need to change for the better into God's likeness.

Some Related Verses Below

We then who are strong ought to bear with the scruples of the weak, and not to please ourselves. (Romans 15:1)

For how do you know, O wife, whether you will save your husband? Or how do you know, O husband, whether you will save your wife? (1 Corinthians 7:16)

Just as I also please all men in all things, not seeking my own profit, but the profit of many, that they may be saved. (1 Corinthians 10:33)

Who is weak, and I am not weak? Who is made to stumble, and I do not burn with indignation? (2 Corinthians 11:29)

CHAPTER 6

Financial Impact

And my God shall supply all your need according
to His riches in glory by Christ Jesus.

—Philippians 4:19

I, like many others, have a great and sincere desire in my heart to win the lost to Jesus. Just from the recollections of the experiences of my own dark past, I know that an intimate relationship with Jesus is the only real answer for others that I observe trapped in sin, sickness, fear, depression, religion, and poverty. One of the obstacles that often seems to hold them back from fulfilling their aspirations is their present financial situation.

Many might be saying, "I want to go on that mission trip," "I want to give for this church outreach," "I want to support that friend going on an overseas team," etc., "I am willing and would do all these desires, but I just don't have the money." They may also be saying, "One day I want to run an overseas orphanage, be a full-time worker to the millions of homeless in Kolkata [Calcutta] living on the streets, but at the moment I just don't have the supply needed to do that."

The Bible says, "God is able to make all grace abound toward you, that you, always having all sufficiency in all things, may have abundance for every good work" (2 Corinthians 9:8). "He supplies seed to the sower, and bread for food" (2 Corinthians 9:10).

Not one of us is really ever ready for the work that God has called us to do (look at the examples in the Bible of the lives of just Moses, Gideon, and Jonah). Not one of these Old Testament patriarchs was ready, equipped, or even really desiring to obey. Sometimes we just need to step out and obey the mighty works of God that He calls us to do.

This pagan church attender first became a Christian way back in the mid-1980s. And while in prayer, I felt the Lord tell me to attend a Christian conference with my family. It was to be held in northern England in the town of Harrogate. The real problem was we didn't have the finances because I had recently changed employment for a much lower income, having just launched out on my own with a new roofing business.

And according to what we had read in the Bible, we were commanded to be out of debt, which we were big time. We had recently cut up our credit cards so as not to use them until we got out of arrears. So there was no way we could really financially plan for all the gas or even be able to reserve a hotel stay for this road trip. A good friend in the church offered us his little tow-behind caravan (trailer), which we parked cheaply with a farmer's permission in a field. We prepared all our own meals, and I had worked out our trip home to the last penny and we could just about make it with an exceedingly tight budget.

We had a great time at the conference, but God's real purpose as to why He brought us there was to learn a valuable lesson about sowing and reaping a harvest. On the last evening, we had just £15 left (a £10 bill and a £5 bill). Here was my plan. Our vehicle was half full of petrol (gas), and I knew we needed £10 extra just to get home safely. Yes, gas was that cheap then. As we put our two young children into the kids' ministry, we arranged with them to meet us outside the conference room in the foyer, and we would get four bags of chips (french fries) from McDonald's before we left for the long road journey back home.

Here was God's plan. During the meeting, a brother shared how he was going to Russia to smuggle in Bibles, and after he had finished speaking, a collection was taken up for this. I felt the Lord's leading to give, but still only had the £10 and £5 notes (bills). As the basket got nearer and nearer, I started to explain to God that if I gave the larger note, we could not get home. And also, if I gave the smaller note, didn't I have a responsibility to my kids, who hadn't eaten since lunch and were even now waiting outside with expectancy for their favorite junk food? I asked the Lord, "Doesn't your word say, 'But if any provide not for his own, and especially for those of his own house, he hath denied the faith, and is worse than an infidel'?" (2 Timothy 5:8).

There was this battle going on in my head, and as the basket came to me, suddenly, on impulse, I dropped both the large and the small bills in! I turned to my wife and told her what I had done and that we couldn't get home. She said, "If God told you to do it [but I wasn't that sure], then we will be fine."

On the way out of the meeting room to face my soon-to-be disappointed kids, I heard a brother I knew call out, "Hey, Malcolm, we're going to McDonald's for supper. We haven't seen you the whole meeting, do you want to join us?" I made some feeble excuse about having to leave now as we had a long drive home, and he repeated, "We really would like you to join us. It's our treat."

I replied, "Are you really sure? There are four of us, you know?"

I had planned a bag of french fries for my kids; God's plan was different. At the restaurant, this dear friend John told my kids to look up at the menu board and said, "Order all you want," and boy, did they! The whole works with milkshakes. I had to brush away a tear as I realized that God wanted to look after my family far better than I ever could. Thank you, John and Nanne, so much. How you have blessed and continue to bless our family and ministry over the years.

Well, after our meal, we said our goodbyes, and now I had to think about how to get home. My plan was to get everyone to sleep in the vehicle while I drove as far as the gas would take us, and then we would get in the trailer and live in it in a rest stop until Tuesday.

This was Sunday night, and on Tuesday morning, I was expecting some money that I could draw out from any local post office.

God's plan was different. About 11:00 p.m., we set off. I drove really slowly, and at around 4:30 a.m., I awoke my family as I pulled into our driveway with still enough gas in the tank to get me to work the next morning.

It was a supernatural miracle! I don't know how God worked that out. I don't need to know. I just rejoiced in him. I had decided not to look at the fuel gauge all the way home and not allow fear to attack my faith. Did we delight ourselves to be in our own beds that early morning? His eye is on the sparrow; how much more does he care for us (Luke 12:7)?

If God has put a vision in your hearts to reach the lost in some way, write it down, keep it before your eyes, stick it on your refrigerator, and talk about it to others. Don't look to your present circumstances and finances or listen to others' negative talk. It is your dream, and it will come to pass. No person, only your own doubts, will keep great things from happening to you and through you. Lack of finances cannot stop it because God's Word says so.

A great way to experience increase ourselves is to sow into another brother's vision, so that there is an overflow in our own. When you perceive that the time is right, step out, take the challenge, trust God's Word, and move on toward your higher calling.

> Think carefully. I am giving you a promise now while the seed is still in the barn. You have not yet harvested your grain, and your grapevines, fig trees, pomegranates, and olive trees have not yet produced their crops. But from this day onward I will bless you. (Haggai 2:18–19 NLT)

Some Related Verses

The Lord is my shepherd; I shall not want."
(Psalm 23:1)

In Him we have redemption through His blood, the forgiveness of sins, according to the riches of His grace. (Ephesians 1:7)

That He would grant you, according to the riches of His glory, to be strengthened with might through His Spirit in the inner man. (Ephesians 3:16)

CHAPTER 7

Beware of Another Jesus

It was in the midsummer of 1985 that, as an established, well-seasoned atheist, I had just been converted one week earlier into a young, new, on-fire baby Christian. So I was very eager to learn more about the Bible. Therefore, when I noticed a Bible exhibition going on from a converted bus in our local village hall's parking lot, my interest was stirred.

After inquiring what it was all about, I was told by a very friendly gentleman that they were about to show a short film about the land of Israel. They said that they also had weekly Bible studies in the very next village to where we lived, and I would be most welcome to join them. The name of this group was "the Christadelphians." We didn't have time at that moment to wait and watch the movie, but I promised to see them on Friday.

Later that evening, I received a telephone call from the missionary whose testimony and teaching witness had led me to accept Jesus Christ as my personal Lord and Savior. He had rung me for a chat and to see how I was doing. I excitedly told him of my great news and the plans to meet with the group called Christadelphians that I had just met and that we would be doing a Bible study with them on Friday evenings. He then revealed to me that he had been planning to start a Bible study group at our home on the exact same night. He said he would really be disappointed if I weren't there and would really like me to be a part of his group, to which I felt I had no choice and reluctantly agreed to open our home on Fridays to his group.

I later on was led to understand that the Christadelphians are a biblical Unitarianism cult that rejects the reality of the Trinity, and that they believe that the immortality of the soul and salvation is obtained through an individual's works on earth.

But the truth is that our salvation has nothing to do with what we have done, but what Jesus alone has done on the cross of Calvary! We can do nothing of ourselves but believe in Jesus. These new friends of ours, Eddie and Annette Martens, were furtively protecting me from deception and another Jesus trying to steal me away from the true Savior and inaccuracies of another religion.

I was at that time just similar to a young oak tree when it is just a small shoot poking through the ground—it can easily be crushed underfoot or eaten by some animal. In the same way, so can the Christian faith be robbed and snuffed out by the enemy of our souls when we are new in the assurance. It is not as easily destroyed after those young shoots become a mighty oak tree. It's the same with the Christian life. How cunning of the enemy to use these dear misguided folks to try and get me off track when I was ignorant of the Word of God and new to the things of eternal salvation.

While being present at one of these recently formed Bible studies at our own home, we were joined one evening by a rather pompous, clerical-collared, mainline denominational minister. He had just arrived back from serving overseas. We were studying the Book of Psalms and the promises of God in them, which was all new and exciting stuff to me.

I was expressing my agreement when this minister, who sounded very wise and mature, totally dampened my enthusiasm. He said that we have to be very careful not to believe all the Bible literally. He said we are far more enlightened these days. He added that the Bible was written by fearful and primitive people in a more superstitious time and much of it was written out of ignorance and trepidation. He went on to repeat that we should be very careful to not personalize the promises of God, especially in the Book of Psalms and Proverbs.

I felt like I had just been beaten over the head with a baseball bat! I was very stunned, to say the least! It was definitely a personal slap in the face! He then went on to ask me if I could possibly believe, for example, that the Bible teaches that the prophet Jonah was swallowed by a great fish. When I answered yes, that's what I did believe, he shook his head in disbelief at my simplistic view of the Bible.

I'm sure he considered me a uneducated country or village bumpkin. Of course, sometime later I learned that Jesus himself confirmed that Jonah was in the great fish for three days: "For as Jonah was three days and three nights in the whale's belly; so shall the Son of man be three days and three nights in the heart of the earth" (Matthew 12:40).

This full-time minister then went on to tell me I was fellowshipping with the wrong people. When I protested at his unloving negativism, he just dismissed me and said I was like a Canute.

King Canute, as most British schoolchildren would have learned, was the Viking king of Norway and Denmark who also became king of England in AD 1016. He is famous for his crazy-believing, idolizing-leading subjects, when they told him he was so powerful he could even stop the incoming ocean tide just by commanding it to stop.

In this ancient historical story, King Canute has to demonstrate to his flattering courtiers that he has no control over the elements (the incoming tide). He was expressing to his followers that secular human power has never been given the power over God's creative power. However, he was sitting on a chair on the beach by the water's edge when the tide started to come in. Of course, all his commanding of the ocean did nothing, and in the end, he had to go back or he would have drowned. Often today, his name is synonymous with anyone ignorantly trying to hold back progress and advancement.

I went to bed that night very despondent and did not get much sleep. I just could not see how I could continue to live this new life if it was just ineffective and not true, as far as the Bible was concerned. Was it either true or false? I was so confused. Oh, I so wanted the Word of God to be the truth for my life. And the recent positive changes in my life which had happened to me had been true enough and real of God. Or were they just achieved by my own strength and wishes?

Well, the very next Sunday, we visited a little Pentecostal church in the Essex village of Debden that we liked attending in the evenings, as our little chapel did not have a service in the evening. They had a guest speaker that night from a Baptist church. I will never forget him as long as I live. His name was Hamish McCrae, a fiery Scottish preacher. He was a professional intellectual, and his IQ (intelligence quota) was very high, so he belonged to Mensa. He was fascinating to watch, for as he preached the Word of God with passion, his unruly long swept-back hair kept falling forward and covering half of his face. I had never seen a preacher like him before and maybe ever since.

I don't remember his subject topic or even his text that night, but right in the middle of his preaching he stopped and held his Bible high and said, "They tell me I am an intellectual mastermind, but I want to tell you all here that I believe every word written in this Bible."

That was good news and music to my ears, for me to hear in my still-confused state of mind. He then went back to his sermon that had nothing to do with what he had just announced. After a little while, he stopped his message once more. With his Bible held high once again he said, "It tells me in this book that Jonah was swallowed by a great fish, and I believe it!" By now I was getting quite excited with what I was hearing from this man of God. The Lord had to be in this!

He went back once again to his sermon and then broke in it one last time. Bible held high again, he declared, "If this Bible says that Jonah ate the great fish I would believe that too."

Now I was fully convinced and could now forever identify with that scripture that says: "For the which cause I also suffer these things: nevertheless, I am not ashamed: for I know whom I have believed and am persuaded that he is able to keep that which I have committed unto him against that day" (2 Timothy 1:12).

That day long ago was for me a genuine supernatural miracle in the Lord's great timing. How wonderful the Holy Spirit is to come to my spiritual rescue in such a dramatic way.

This preacher was a super intellectual, and yet he publicly confessed that he believed the whole written Bible as God's Word. I never did have a chance to tell Hamish McCrae the effect his ministry had on me that day because, at that time, I didn't have the nerve to get up and speak to the (big) speakers. I had heard once that a big speaker is just a small speaker away from home. (LOL)

I wondered if, when he got back home to Scotland, he ever questioned himself about why he had spoken about Jonah, as it was completely unrelated to his preached sermon. It was just for me, and I knew it. Never again would I doubt the Word of God. Never again would I let someone else confuse me on this subject. I was set free. I now believe that God is so powerful he could even stop the mighty ocean just by commanding it to. Or He can even stop the sun and moon for twenty-four hours if He needs to. In fact, what do you know? He did!

> Then Joshua spoke to the Lord in the day when the Lord delivered up the Amorites before the children of Israel, and he said in the sight of Israel: "Sun, stand still over Gibeon; And moon, in the Valley of Aijalon." So, the sun stood still, and the moon stopped, till the people had revenge Upon their enemies. Is this not written in the Book of Jasher? So, the sun stood still in the midst of heaven, and did not hasten to go down for about a whole day and there has been no day like that, before it or after it, that the Lord heeded the voice of a man; for the LORD fought for Israel. (Joshua 10:12–14).

Some Related Verses

> For the word of God is quick, and powerful, and sharper than any two-edged sword, piercing even to the dividing asunder of soul and spirit, and of the joints and marrow, and is a dis-

cerner of the thoughts and intents of the heart.
(Hebrews 4:12)

All scripture is given by inspiration of
God, and is profitable for doctrine, for reproof,
for correction, for instruction in righteousness.
(2 Timothy 3:16)

CHAPTER 8

A Supernatural God

One reason we, as Christians, are not blessed with many of the promises God has guaranteed us in his Word is because we don't hear or obey the voice of God. He (Jesus) replied, "Blessed rather are those who hear the Word of God and obey it" (Luke 11:28).

One explanation for this is that although we hear it, we are not really listening to it. Other times, it's because we close our ears to the word of God, thinking it will be too challenging for us. But the following verse says that those who hear and obey God find it uncomplicated, and they will be blessed. Jesus said, "For my yoke is easy and my burden is light" (Matthew 11:30).

Some Christians really believe that if they listen to God, they might just end up in some remote cannibal's cooking pot in the darkest Africa. I'm stretching that a bit there, but that really couldn't be further from the truth.

There is a solution or a positive answer in God's Word for every one of our questions, our situations, and every single problem we may have in this life. "I will give you the keys of the kingdom of heaven; whatever you bind on earth will be bound in heaven, and whatever you loose on earth will be loosed in heaven" (Matthew 16:19).

God is a supernatural Spirit and wants to do great things in us and through us. If only we would recognize his voice and obey it. God is looking for us to make an impact on those around us for Jesus and to bless us at the same time. God speaks through the Bible first, but he also speaks to us all the time through everyday things, if only we would listen and understand him.

The actual first personal short-term mission trip our family went on was to Eastern Europe. It was just after the communist parties started falling in all these USSR satellite countries. Many churches in the United Kingdom were feeling led to go and help with the great needs, particularly in Romania.

At that time, I was asked to be a part of one such team but declined, telling the team leader that I believed we were being led to go to Czechoslovakia. Although for the most part, at that time, I didn't even know where that specific country was located. It all started when we felt challenged to start praying for that country, maybe because at that time we were driving a tiny used Škoda 120 Estelle car made in Czechoslovakia.

In 1992, Phyllis and I joined a group from the Full Gospel Business Men's Fellowship International on a trip to Israel, but that would be a whole other story. While in Jerusalem, we visited the sparse inventoried Scripture Union Book Store in the city center. Besides Hebrew and English Bibles on the shelves, there were three Bibles in a language I didn't know.

On inquiring, I was informed they were Czech scriptures. I immediately felt impressed to buy them and to believe that I would put these books from that country into three citizens' hands one day in Czechoslovakia. Supernatural miracle number one had been birthed by faith!

Just a few weeks later, an American Christian from New England in the USA telephoned me in the UK. He said that he had just returned from Israel and had been with the same tour guide, Tony John, as we had had. He said that Tony had told him that we were believing to visit Czechoslovakia one day. He informed me that he would be leading a small team there in a couple of weeks and invited us to meet up with him and his team in Prague, the capital, on a certain date in just fifteen days at 7:00 p.m. (time zone GMT+2). The address he gave us had to be spelled out to me letter by letter over the telephone, as neither of us could even pronounce it.

At that particular time, our roofing business was in a slump because of a nationwide recession. My wife and I couldn't see how we could possibly go, as we were behind in our mortgage payment and our credit cards at that time were maxed out. We even had to struggle for gas to get to church on the following Sunday.

While we were there, we did ask our Australian pastors, Rod Frankland and his wife Hazel, privately for prayer and for their advice and direction. To our utter surprise, he stood up as the service ended that evening and announced to his congregation about our proposed trip. He held up a £100 note (bill), which he declared was from him and his wife Hazel, and said, "Let's start a collection and send the Blowes family off on their first short-term mission trip."

On the ride home, we rejoiced that we were heading into Eastern Europe, wherever that was. We still had need of personal finances back at our home and business, but our church members had given everything we needed for our trip to that distant country of Czechoslovakia. As young Christians, we had never seen anything like that happen before. Supernatural miracle 2! We were soon informed by the US team leader, Dave Wells, that on the first day of the team tour, we were to meet with the current USA ambassador to that country, Shirley Temple Black, the former Hollywood child movie star.

So the following week, my wife Phyllis, our two youngest kids Samuel and Holly, and I set off on this great adventure in our company box van. We prepared to drive for two days. We started first by taking the ferry from Felixstowe, Suffolk, and debarking in Calais, in northern France. We had never been to nor driven in Europe before, and I had to learn to drive on the left side of the road in our right-hand drive vehicle.

We drove right across Europe from France, through Belgium, to Germany, and on into Czechoslovakia and to the capital, Prague, very early the next morning. We had some difficulties at each border because we had packed our van with things to help the broken country we were heading to. Everybody seemed to want money, and at the Czech border, we suspected that they wanted a bribe. We didn't speak French, German, or Czech at that time.

We told them that they were gifts and were to be given out free. I remember one border inspector saying, "Nothing in this world is free, my friend." We were like fish out of water. It was like we had just gotten off the banana boat. However, we got through these borders mostly unscathed.

We arrived very early in the morning in the capital, Prague, and with all the holdups, we had missed our meeting date by one day and the time for the first evening encounter. We were tired, hungry, and had driven a long way but decided to press on anyway. Not one person that we approached for directions seemed to speak any English.

Prague is a massive city, and we showed this address to multiple taxi drivers and asked about it, showing the slip of paper to people all day. No one could help or understand us. There was a time when there was no GPS, street signs, or maps available in this ex-communist country. By the end of the day, I was getting very frustrated.

I said to my wife and two young children, "This is ridiculous! I am tired, I'm hungry, I'm smelly, and we're lost and on a wild goose chase. We have missed it, and I am going back home."

I was so lost that it took us over an hour traveling around in the city to just try and find the road back to Germany. I had to confess to my family that I had no idea where I was. Suddenly a little Škoda car cut right across our path.

"Look at that vehicle's number plate!" I declared. "That is a scripture. Look it up."

My wife replied, "That's stupid," but she looked it up anyway. The plate was ACT.9.6-7. It said, "But get up and enter the city, and it will tell you what you must do. The men who traveled with him stood speechless" (NASB). Tremendous supernatural miracle 3!

We both immediately knew we had just heard a personal *rhema* word of God, so I turned our van around and started heading back into the city center that we could now just see some miles in the distance. Returning once again to the city center, we started to ask once more, but nonetheless got the same results as before.

After a while, I decided on a different and maybe unwise strategy, which was to park our van on a street and start inquiring again on foot. Searching again for directions to this address and wandering for about an hour, we were not only lost again; but this time, we couldn't even find our way back to our vehicle and had no clue where we had left it. All the streets and apartment blocks looked the same.

We came upon another parked little taxi car and showed him our ruffled piece of paper. He beckoned us to get in the back of his little car. What other choices did we have? After driving for a while, we suddenly went past our van. I couldn't decide whether to let the driver keep going or to stop and not lose it again. I told my family to try and remember the directions from it.

We needn't have been concerned, as the decision was made for us. We came to a stop just around the corner from where our van was parked. The taxi driver pointed to a big church building and to my paper address. From outside, we could hear preaching in English, and as we made our way inside, there were the Americans, and we were on our way to our first most remarkable mission trip.

I had a good friend back in England who is now with the Lord Jesus in heaven. He was a Christian, an intellectual, a scientist, and a professor and had been awarded an honor personally by Charles, Prince of Wales (now King Charles III of England). He declared that through that incident in Prague, we had proved that there was a God because the odds of a car with a plate in the form of a scripture that answered the very thing we needed, at the very time we needed it were billions to one against.

God is supernatural and wants to communicate with us daily and bless us. Be expectant to hear from God today and be determined to obey and receive the blessing that God wants to give you right now.

Some Related Verses

Behold, I am the Lord, the God of all flesh;
is anything too difficult for Me? (Jeremiah 32:27)

And looking at them, Jesus said to them,
With people this is impossible, but with God all
things are possible. (Matthew 19:6)

CHAPTER 9

We Are One in Him

Bear one another's burdens, and so fulfill the law of Christ.

—Galatians 6:2

B ecause of the reality of the above scripture, we can sing, shout, dance, and rejoice in times of trouble and tribulation because we know our God will make a way out for us.

I am not going to be persuaded by what I feel, what I hear, or what I see! I am motivated by what I believe and what God's Word says! Certainly, this next account helped me and perhaps may also help you, the reader, to adopt this same attitude.

I want to give a personal testimony to a most remarkable and exceedingly supernatural occurrence. It was all in the Lord's exact timing, and it took place on one occasion in my life while on the overseas mission field.

In 1994, my wife, our two youngest kids Samuel and Holly, and I were living in the recently formed country of the Republic of Slovakia.

Prior to this move from England, I had been very much involved, as a Christian businessman, with the Full Gospel Business Men's Fellowship International (FGBMFI). So it was only natural that I would continue to promote and start chapters in the new country in which we now resided.

In the summer of that year, the fellowship in the United Kingdom announced a date for a men's conference up in the north of England, and we prayed and felt it right to attend. It was to be a long drive, but our Nissan van was only a few years old, had low mileage, and we were sure it would make it there and back with no trouble over the 2,500-mile round trip.

We decided to first drive to Prague, the capital city of the Czech Republic, and pick up some of the Czechoslovakian FGBMFI members whom we had become acquainted with and take them with us as guests.

The first stage of our journey was that on arriving at the city of a hundred spires, we had already driven 240 miles, and it was still another 990 plus miles to our destination.

Our planned route was to go all the way across Germany, entering Belgium, and finally to arrive at the Belgium channel port of Zeebrugge. From there, we planned to take the ferry, which we had prebooked along with our vehicle. This would take us to the English port of Felixstowe in the county of Suffolk and then on to the north of England.

After sleeping the night at a Christian brother's home in Prague, we set off early the next morning. We had driven about four hours and had put about another 260 miles behind us and were happily on our way on the E50 German autobahn. Unexpectedly, I felt that our engine was starting to have a loss of power. Looking into the rearview mirror, I saw a blue cloud of smoke following us. Suddenly, there was a loud bang, and we came to an abrupt halt.

We were right by the exit ramp (*Ausfahrt*) for the town of Würzburg. We manually pushed our vehicle out of the fast-moving highway onto the hard shoulder and then down the off-ramp into a gas station parking lot.

We were stranded with no backup plan! We had no idea how to get help or what we needed. None of our group could even speak much German. All we could do was pray, but praying for God's wisdom turned out to be all we needed!

We stayed with the vehicle for hours, hoping someone might stop and give us some help. The Czech brothers didn't seem to realize the gravity of our situation and saw it as an opportunity to write on big sheets of paper in Czech "JESUS LOVES YOU" and stand up on the side of the highway waving these placards at the traffic! By midafternoon, we were hot, tired, hungry, exhausted, overwhelmed, and despondent.

Suddenly, a thought came to me. I had a couple of German-language FGBMFI *Voice* magazines (*Stimme*) in our van's glove compartment. I had put them there in the hope of handing them out if I had an opportunity when we stopped for gas. These magazines in every language always had a list of the towns in their own country where fellowship chapters had been set up. I looked up the German list, and yes, there was a chapter in the city of Würzburg and a telephone number. Was this God's answer for asked wisdom?

With sign language, I persuaded the gas station attendant to use the company phone (no cellphones then) to ring that local number. Reluctantly, he rang the number and handed me the phone. A man answered in German, and I asked if he spoke English. He answered in perfect but broken English. He introduced himself as Heinz Schubert and said he was the fellowship's chapter president.

I explained our dire situation. He asked where we were stranded and said he would send a vehicle to pick us all up and bring us to his house. He was as good as his word, and what a relief it was to be welcomed into his home by him and his beautiful wife, Evi.

We were all suffering from the day's heat; we were fatigued, famished, and dirty. We were given a wonderful German meal and then offered, as complete strangers, a shower and a bed for the night in their large house.

I needed to sleep, so we went to bed early, and as we lay resting in the dark of that delightfully cool cellar room, I said to Phyllis, "I don't know what we will do tomorrow. We will miss our ferry, and somehow we must try to just get back to Czechoslovakia. As for the vehicle, probably we would have to just dump it, although we were going to need a vehicle when we got back home."

I said, "We must trust God, not worry, and recognize he has gotten us in his hands." We reminded ourselves of the scripture that states, "Cast your burden on the Lord, and He shall sustain you; He shall never permit the righteous to be moved" (Psalm 55:22).

Unbeknown to us, that late evening, Heinz started to telephone many of the different churches he had contact with in the city. Obviously, he got a negative reaction from most of the fellowships.

Incredibly, the Roman Catholic Church offered to loan us their twelve-seat church minibus. It gave me an adjusted perspective on that particular church denomination. They certainly knew and walked in the scripture, "Bear one another's burdens, and so fulfill the law of Christ" (Galatians 6:2).

I never want to confess unbelief, but it was genuinely astonishing when Heinz informed us in the morning and took us outside to show us this vehicle. It literally took my breath away.

I asked how they could just trust us, as complete foreign strangers, to go off into another country overseas with their near-brand-new vehicle and be sure we would ever bring it back or see us again. They even gave us money for gas. It was truly a miracle! We went back inside and had coffee and a delicious Bavarian breakfast.

I then told our group that if we hurried, it was still plausible that we could make the ferry on time. It was now a lot easier for me than my own van because now I was driving a left-hand vehicle on the right side of the highways. Before, I was driving a right-hand vehicle on the right side of the road. It also had passenger windows all around, which our van didn't, so it was a blessing in more ways than one.

I then expressed again my previously concerned thoughts to my wife. "Let's just go and not be anxious about the situation and enjoy ourselves in England and figure out what to do when we get back to Würzburg and return the Catholic church's vehicle."

Well, we just made it to the ferry on time, enjoyed a great time in the United Kingdom at the conference, and visited churches, family, and friends. After a couple of weeks, we caught the ferry back to Belgium and then on to Heinz and Evi's home in Würzburg.

We were welcomed back with open arms and with some incredible news. Apparently, some months before, the different city churches had gotten together and had organized a concessions stand for the Billy Graham live-link meeting. "Behold, how good and how pleasant it is for brethren to dwell together in unity! For there, the Lord commanded the blessing, life forevermore" (Psalm 133).

They had made a big profit from this and were not sure what to do with the money. While we were in the UK, they prayed and decided it was the Lord's will to put a good used engine in our vehicle while we were away, and when we arrived back, there it was, our vehicle standing in the driveway looking like new again.

Wow. Let me say it backward: wow. Let's turn that frown upside down. What could I say to justify such love to us? It was another miracle. "Bear one another's burdens, and so fulfill the law of Christ" (Galatians 6:2).

England and Germany have had some real issues in our parents' generation and many conflicts with each other because of World War II, but Heinz and Evi became our dearest firm friends. Every time we went on a trip back to the UK, we would always stop and stay with them on the way there and again on the way back to break up our journey.

One time we stopped there, and they saw our tires were getting bald and replaced them for us while we slept. On another planned visit, we telephoned ahead and told them we were coming. They said on that particular date, they would be away, but they would leave the door key to their spectacular empty house with the next-door neighbor for us to use. What trust!

There is one more miracle to finish this story off. On another visit, when our then fifteen-year-old son Samuel had said to me one day that he would like a special, expensive pair of tennis shoes (trainers), I replied, "I am so sorry, son. Your earthly father doesn't have the money for them. You will have to ask your heavenly Father for them."

Soon after, on the next stopover and visit to the Schuberts' home, because we were full-time missionaries, they showed us a room in their cellar full of clothes they had collected, which they themselves were taking into the earlier fallen communist countries. They said to us, "Take anything you need or can use." Okay, you've probably guessed it by now. Yes, there they were, the exact pair of almost-new trainers in Sam's precise size! Samuel and Holly had a great time pulling out other shoes and clothes that they wanted that day.

The Christians of Würzburg certainly showed us their love of God through their generosity and their practicing the fruits of the Holy Spirit.

Some Related Verses

The fruit of the Spirit is love, joy, peace, longsuffering, kindness, goodness, faithfulness, gentleness, self-control. Against such, there is no law. (Galatians 5:22–23)

What is the exceeding greatness of His power toward us who believe, according to the working of His mighty power. (Ephesians 1:19)

He himself shall dwell in prosperity, and his descendants shall inherit the earth. (Psalm 25:13)

CHAPTER 10

Does God Need Our Faith?

Our ministry, Win Our Nations, Inc. (founded in the United Kingdom in 1986), has been set up and officially registered in the country of India for twenty-two years. We went there for the first time in 1998 and have led many short-term team visits and longer personal stays for the past twenty years.

It is a country exceptionally different from many others we have been to. Today it has significantly advanced in many areas, even into the more rural tribal areas.

When we first went there, it was their summer period, and there was often a blistering heat (127 degrees Fahrenheit in the shade one time!). There was no air conditioning, plus there was the incredibly spicy food of the south that we had to get accustomed to. That means for breakfast, lunch, and dinner!

The first few years we visited, there was almost no access to a connecting overseas telephone except in the major cities. With the primitive ablutions, it made it very hard for many of our visiting western team members. When entering for the first time, most participants either genuinely treasured their time there, and a few really loathed it. India seems to have no middle ground in the thoughts of most western hemisphere folk; they either fall in love with India or they hate it.

We have had both those types on the different short-term mission teams that we have led there in the past. They all had to get used to the lack of readily available sanitation, plus the sights and odors. Photographs or videos can never capture the smells of India, which you start to experience almost from the moment of disembarkation from the airplane.

I think God has given Phyllis and me a supernatural love for that subcontinent because we are now fully accustomed to the heat and aromas and find their appetizing curried cuisine deliciously sought-after.

Apart from the official anti-Christian government officers, we have always found that the everyday Indian population, whether they are Muslim, Hindu, or of a Christian faith, is warm, welcoming, and friendly to visitors.

When we first visited India, our plan was to hold outreach evangelism meetings in remote villages. But by 2001, we had become concerned. The souls that gave their lives to Jesus Christ in these meetings had no training and often just went immediately out to start evangelizing without having even the most basic Christian teaching.

Our India coordinator said the real answer was to start a residential Bible college with a two-year program. I confess at that time I had not the faintest idea or the finances on how to go about such a need. Our daughter Holly gave us $25. I said, "What is that for?" She replied, "For your Bible college in India." I said, "We don't have a Bible college in India."

We got the message, and so we decided to start an account for this project and put aside any surplus we had. After about two years, we had a grand total of just a little over $860 saved toward it.

As a brief sidenote, it is an interesting fact that Holly and her husband Jake, after living full-time in the country of Cameroon for twenty years, have started a WON Bible college there.

Back to that previous time. Andrew Wommack, a Bible teacher with his own Bible school from Colorado Springs, was to be a guest speaker at our local church over a three-day period. He spoke about needing to expand by buying new property for his own ministry.

Before he arrived, our church pastor said to the congregation that he was believing for fifty members to give $1,000 so the church would be able to present him with a minimum gift of $50,000.

I had never heard of such a thing before. But incredibly, I sensed from God that he was speaking to me and that we were to be one of those fifty givers. Our financially tight missionary lifestyle that we lived never gave us that sort of mentality and faith to give so much at one time before. We had worked up from $25 to $50 above our 10 percent tithe, and now we thought of ourselves as super spiritual from time to time giving $100. But a thousand, wow!

I immediately reminded God in case he didn't know that I had two problems with that directive. One was, What would my wife sitting next to me say? And two was that we didn't have the needed money. As we walked out of the church, I casually mentioned to my wife that I thought the Lord was calling us to be one of those fifty $1,000 sowers. To my great surprise, she told me she felt the same. Problem 1 solved. So I asked her how she thought we could get the money.

I unwisely suggested putting it on a credit card, to which she said at once, "*No*, we are not going back down that road."

Before we became Christians, we were always maxed out on our credit cards. After our salvation, we had cut them all up, and it had taken us a couple of years to get out of their clutches. We couldn't think of anything we owned that we could sell for that much.

At one previous time, our pastor in England's son was getting married, and we didn't have the money for the petrol for the forty-mile round trip. We had believed that God would somehow supernaturally give us the money. So my wife, the kids, and I showered and dressed in our best and waited and waited until the time the wedding had started, but no cash came.

We sadly missed that great day, but we never went back into debt over it. We accepted it as a test of whether we would borrow it again or not. The Bible informs us that we are to "owe no one anything but love" (Romans 13:8).

It also tells us that "the borrower is servant to the lender" (Proverbs 22:7). We certainly didn't want to come under the control again of unholy institutions that could demand whatever they wanted from us in charges and interest payments.

Years later, when we told our pastor about that situation, he said we should have telephoned him, and he would have given us money for petrol (gas). But as usual, my stupid pride had gotten in the way.

I knew all we had to spare was the $860 in the India Bible college account, and it had taken us a good while to get that amount. I had come to believe and understand the principle that if what we had didn't meet the need, then it must be seed.

So I suggested to my wife, "Then let's find the remainder of the money somehow to make up to the desired amount and sow our college fund into Andrew's Bible school for our own." Therefore, this is what we did, and we whooped ("God loves a cheerful giver," 2 Corinthians 9:7) as we sowed our $1,000 check into the offering basket.

I am still unable to put my finger upon just how it all happened, but in less than two months later, we were both in India. We had rented a large building, borrowed a truck, and went out and bought twenty desks, chairs, and beds; a computer; and all office equipment. Plus, all kitchen equipment and food needed to feed the students.

And we had eighteen tribal students with full sponsorship support for their first year! We sure realized that God is ready to use our faith from that lesson.

Every year, we have led one and in some years two USA short-term adult teams to India. And every year, our India coordinator would take the team to visit vacant land that was for sale, and we would pray over it, and that was about all. A good piece of arable land with around five acres at that time was around $50,000 to $60,000.

I guess I didn't really have the faith about how we were ever going to get our Bible college, future orphanage, and elementary school out of rented buildings.

Back in the States one time, I bumped into a recent India team member, Pastor Bryan Moore, who asked me, "Malcolm, have you got that land in India yet?" I made some feeble excuse to him about "still working on it." Immediately from that brief encounter, I suddenly realized it was my unbelief holding back the purchase of land in India. "Lord, I believe; help my unbelief!" (Mark 9:24).

When I got back to our office, I declared to my wife, "Phyllis, we need to repent of our unbelief and complacency and of just doing nothing to claim our land in India."

We then did nothing material about raising the money needed except to repent and continue to pray without ceasing. Just *one* week later, someone walked into our office with a check for $30,000. A few days later, a check for another $15,000 came in. And so it continued for another $15,000 in smaller amounts.

We bought over four acres of super-arable land in the village of Bhogapuram, Andhra Pradesh, Southeast India.

We soon started construction of buildings after the purchase, and today it houses our Bible college and the students' classrooms, dormitories, kitchen, and dining hall. It also has our orphanage and an elementary school for 150 young students.

Just as a side note, I believe our faith is also used in the ministry of physical healing. Many years ago, while still living in England, I had a call from a good friend, a Christian farmer named Tony Gardiner who lived some eighty miles away. A young man, Barry Cavanaugh*, from Tony's own village, had been given a diagnosis of a terminal brain tumor.

They were going to operate on him at Addenbrooke's Hospital in Cambridge, and as it was near where we lived, Tony wondered if we could go and pray for him.

When we got to his hospital room, a nun was just leaving. His wife was at his bedside in a distraught state, and Barry was unconscious. They had shaved his head and had drawn many marker lines on it in preparation for his operation later that day.

I introduced myself and told his wife that we were born-again Christians and that we had seen many miracles take place after prayer. We then asked her if we may anoint her husband with oil, lay hands on him, and pray for him, to which she consented. We did these and left.

We gave it a couple of days and returned to his ward and find his room empty. When we inquired about him, a nurse informed us

---

* Name changed to protect the person.

that he had gone home. We thought she meant he had died. "No, no," she said. "He has been discharged and released and has gone home."

I telephoned Tony, who inquired about Barry. His wife said he was, at that time, down the public house having a beer!

Let me ask, Did God need my faith? Not really at all, but he deemed to use it anyway.

> But without faith it is impossible to please
> Him, for he who comes to God must believe that
> He is, and that He is a rewarder of those who
> diligently seek Him (Hebrews 11:6)

Even Jesus could do little without faith to work in his own town of Nazareth. "Now He could do no mighty work there, except that He laid His hands on a few sick people and healed them. And He marveled because of their unbelief" (Mark 6:5–6). So have faith in God!

Faith is mentioned 391 times in the New King James Bible version.

Have faith in God!

Some Related Verses

> Now faith is the substance of things hoped
> for, the evidence of things not seen. (Hebrews
> 11:1)

> The just shall live by faith. (Habakkuk 2:4)

BIBLIOGRAPHY

The publications I have read, studied, and quoted in the writing of this book.

Unless otherwise stated, all the Bible quotes are from the New King James Bible (NKJV).

- The Oxford English Dictionary
- Wikipedia
- Dr. Bill Winston Ministries
- *Plane & Pilot* (March 2023)
- Copyright 2005 Sol Luckman
- *Limitless Love: A 365 Day Devotion* by Kenneth and Gloria Copeland
- *Will Rogers: Wise and Witty Sayings of a Great American Humorist* by Art Wortman
- "7 Unexpected Side Effects of Surgical Abortion" (https://www.beautyepic.com/surgical-abortion-side-effects)
- Success.com
- Tinseltownmom.com
- Rick Warren quotes

Malcolm Blowes, PhD, is currently the international director of Win Our Nations, Inc., and has been a full-time missionary since 1992. He initially served the Lord Jesus full-time for five and a half years in the Republic of Slovakia. After this, he left for the USA to join Teen Missions International Inc. as their India coordinator for three years. After completing that in the year 2000, he returned as the director of Win Our Nations, Inc., working from their USA base in Cocoa, Florida. He currently copastors Faith Family Fellowship Church, which he founded in Cocoa.

Malcolm has been married to his wife, Phyllis, for fifty-four years and has been a born-again Christian since the summer of 1985, when his life was dramatically transformed as he came to the saving knowledge of Jesus Christ and received God's amazing love and mercy through the ministry of another missionary couple.

They have four children: Daniel, Benjamin, Samuel, and Holly. They also have nine grandchildren: Joshua, Seth, Jude, Jordan, William, Amy, Ellie, Joel, and Spencer.

The missionary life keeps them busy as they travel the globe sharing the good news of Jesus Christ. God has called them to set up churches, orphanages, and Bible schools to raise up and care for nationals in the knowledge of the Lord Jesus and God's Word. They have set up children's homes in India and Cameroon, Africa, and also an elementary school and a residential Bible college in India. They have bought land in both countries. They have seen many miracles and healings through their ministry.

Malcolm and Phyllis firmly believe that *missions* are the heartbeat of God, and their desire is to encourage and make the body of Christ aware of their own responsibilities.